Coffee, Cookies, and Propofol

Paralyzed by Sedation—the True Story of Sandra Smith

Denise Smith

Coffee, Cookies, and Propofol

First Printing, 2017

ISBN-13: 978-1978443198

ISBN: 1978443196

Library Control of Congress Number: 2017917838
LCCN Imprint Name: CreateSpace Independent Publishing Platform, North Charleston, SC

www.CoffeeCookiesandPropofol.com

Coffee, Cookies, and Propofol

Thank You from Sandy

We all know it takes a village to raise a child. I feel like it took a village to save my life.

I am grateful to the following people:

My daughter, Denise; my granddaughter, Brandy; and my son, Billy, for making me go to the hospital, or I would not be here today.

The Slatington Police Department.

The EMTs from Northern Valley Emergency Medical Services (NOVA) who got me to Blue Mountain Health System (old Palmerton Hospital) alive.

Everyone at Blue Mountain Health System (BMHS) ER for keeping me alive.

The Lehighton transport team who got me to St. Luke's Bethlehem through the atrocious Route 22 traffic.

Coffee, Cookies, and Propofol

Everyone at St. Luke's for everything they did in the Medical Intensive Care Unit (MICU).

Anyone who also worked on February 17 on either ambulance, in the BMHS ER, at St. Luke's Bethlehem MICU, and all the doctors.

Bob and Sue—a special thank you for taking care of my house and my cat.

Alice Wanamaker for your continued support.

Mandy Bolton for all your assistance.

Thank you very much for my life back.

Coffee, Cookies, and Propofol

Dedication

To all those who suffer from post-traumatic

stress disorder

Coffee, Cookies, and Propofol

Table of Contents

Coffee, Cookies, and Propofol

Preface

My name is Sandra Smith. A bit about me: I am a redhead with green eyes and a banging body. Just kidding. I am sixty-eight years old, stand about five feet five inches tall, and have brown hair and brown eyes. I was born and raised in a small town in Northeastern Pennsylvania nestled between the Appalachian Mountains and the valley of the Lehigh River—Palmerton. I am my parents' only daughter, with three older brothers. I attended Stephen S. Palmer High School, where I met my husband, Bill. We got married when I was twenty years old and Bill had recently returned home from serving in the war in Vietnam. Our family grew by two with the birth of my daughter, Denise, followed by my son, Billy Jr., in the early seventies. When Billy was about three years old and Denise about five years old, we moved a few miles away to Slatington,

Pennsylvania.

Not too long after Billy was born, I developed
rashes on my skin. I was diagnosed with psoriasis and,
soon after, rheumatoid arthritis. This was back in the good
old days before the common knowledge that these were
autoimmune diseases. Thinking it was solely a skin
disorder, my doctors began treatment. We started with
creams applied in a regimented fashion—first by rubbing
the area raw, then applying the ointment before lying in
the sun for six hours, and then spending six hours in a
darkened room. Luckily, I was a homemaker, because the
rigorous schedule did not allow for much else. Then came
the steroids in various forms of pills and graduating to
injections—all the while still applying those creams. When
there was not much success, we upgraded to UVB lights. I
had a UVB booth installed in my house for the daily burns,
or treatments. Of all the treatments, my least favorite was

the tar. Yes, I had to smear tar all over my body and then burn under the UVB lights. I was burned to a crisp, but there was slight improvement. Through all this I remembered a comment one of my older brothers made before he passed away: "Don't ever let 'em get you down. You can handle it." And handle it I did. But nothing prepared me for what was coming.

As with all medications, something new was right around the corner. Someone discovered that these conditions were autoimmune related, and biologicals were invented! Enbrel. It was like a miracle—two shots that I could take weekly at home with virtually no side effects. As my breathing worsened, a newer medication would make things even easier—just a pill two times a day.

As my experimental treatments continued, Denise and Billy were simultaneously raising children of their own, together blessing Bill and me with five grandchildren. We were married thirty-six years before Bill passed away in

1998. His passing and the passing of time brought our family closer together. Denise, Billy, and my granddaughter, Brandy, all live on the family property and as such are very close, and I wouldn't have it any other way. My daughter and I now do almost everything together. What I don't do with her, I do with Brandy. Billy is around most of the time and stops in to say hi and check on me several times a day.

I have never been one to attend church. I do believe in God and feel that I can speak to Him anytime, anywhere. I always try to be a good person and to help whoever I can. I try to be fair and not to lie, except maybe those little white lies about haircuts and outfits so as not to cause hurt feelings. I am always there to support friends and family in any way possible. I like to be busy. I would much rather be doing something, as it drives me crazy to sit still for too long. I worked part time, had a hot supper on the table, baked goodies for the kids, kept a clean house, and still had time for my husband and children. As any wife knows, this is like having several full-time jobs.

When I got married and took the vow "till death us do part," I never realized for how many people this is true. Death will part you. Someone will be left alone. I was heartbroken. My best friend was gone. Whom would I talk to now? I went through the range of grieving emotions, but a bit of anger lingered. I was mad that he left me alone, mad that he refused to see the doctor before it was too late, mad that he kept his illness a secret for so long. Mostly I was mad at myself for not picking up on the symptoms, for not pushing the issue when I noticed he was not quite right. Why did I let him procrastinate? Later I would learn that I was the exact same way, procrastinating until I nearly lost my life.

I had to return to work full time after Bill passed away. I took a job at a local Laundromat and dry cleaner. It did not pay well, and I worked a lot of long hours. In

2004, an X-ray showed a lump in my lung. After many tests, they determined it was dried blood and calcium and we would monitor the situation every six months. There was nothing more to do as long as the lump did not change. It is still there and has not grown at all over the years.

In 2006, I was diagnosed with chronic obstructive pulmonary disease (COPD), proving that smoking no less than a pack of cigarettes a day catches up to you eventually. I didn't have time to be sick. I am sure everyone feels that way at one time or another. If you need money for all of the things in life one needs to pay for, which I did, you get up every day and you go to work. It does not matter how bad you feel. That was me. I would work between forty and fifty hours a week because I had bills to pay. Most banks and debtors don't understand or care how bad you feel; they want to get paid.

About the beginning of 2009, my grandson Billy III, who lived with me at the time, decided to move out and could not take his cat along to his new place. So, guess what? I inherited a cat. I named him Pudders, and he became my baby. Pudders never missed a cuddle. From day one, as soon as I sat on my recliner, he was on my lap, and we would nap.

In January of 2010, I became very ill and was in and out of the hospital three times in three months. It was due to my COPD. Each time I got ill, it took me a little longer to get back on my feet both physically and financially.

In the days before my husband died, the doctor told us if anyone wanted to see him one last time, that time was now. The osteopathic philosophy is that systems of the body are interrelated, each working with the other to heal in times of illness. The same ideology holds true for family systems. When one member of the family is ill, it may take all parts of the family to heal or at the very least cope effectively. When another family member died a few years later, the family all gathered together. In both of these instances, the hospital provided a cart with coffee, tea, and cookies for the family. This is a kind gesture to ensure you may not have to leave your loved one's side. It brings comfort and aids in the bonding and sharing of strength during a difficult or lengthy illness or impending death. Over the years, I had forgotten about this. But when I heard it again, it all came rushing back to me.

Two years later my COPD had progressed to a point where I needed more regular care and had to be hospitalized. Upon my release, nearly three weeks later, I had to be on oxygen full time. I was unable to continue to work. That year was rough on me financially. By the end of 2012, I had been treated by a lot of different doctors for a variety of diseases and syndromes. By the time 2014 rolled around, my health was improving. I was getting better, and I made plans to take a trip to Las Vegas. I had always wanted to go, and I thought I should before my health got worse again. Well I never got there. I ended up in the hospital for eleven days and missed my vacation. It was another flare-up of my COPD.

Over the last fifty years, I have been put to sleep many times for various medical procedures—everything from having a tooth pulled to having surgery on my elbow. I never had a problem or experience like the one you are about to read.

Propofol is a short acting sedative - hypnotic agent used as a general anesthetic. It is administered by intravenous to sedate a patient, often used in critical care patients requiring intubation by a mechanical ventilator (breathing machine).

Typical initial dosing for ICU Sedation: 5 mcg/kg/min for intubated mechanically ventilated patients.

Maintenance dosing: May increase in 5 to 10 mcg/kg/min increments every 5 minutes. Typical maintenance dosing range is 5 to 50 mcg/kg/min.

Chapter 1

Saved

I remember not feeling well as early as the tenth but
became very sick by the fourteenth or fifteenth of February
2017. My symptoms included the typical fatigue,
congestion, etc. This was nothing new; my COPD would
usually flare up in the winter months at least once a year.
My daughter called our family doctor right away and made
an appointment for the next morning. We have learned
that if I feel sick in the morning, by the afternoon the
situation usually escalates so quickly that I am hospital
bound. I go from feeling bad—"one" on the scale—to really
sick—"ten" on the scale—in no time at all. Lucky for me I
have a very diligent care team. When I am unable to get in
to see the doctor, he calls in a prescription to Bechtel's,
our local pharmacy, so I'll have the antibiotic or steroid I

need until I can get in to see him. This was the case that day in mid-February. My family doctor called in an antibiotic and started me on steroids.

By the next day, the medicines had begun to work, and I didn't really feel sick anymore. I was just physically and mentally exhausted. I thought if I went back to bed to sleep for a little while and continued on the medication, I would feel better. February seventeenth was much of the same. When I woke up and got out of bed, I still felt tired. I just wanted to sleep. I honestly do not remember ever being so tired in my entire life.

Denise stopped in before she went to work that morning—like she does every morning—to check on me and see how I was doing. She wasn't too thrilled with what she saw in me and thought I had worsened to the point where it was time to call for an ambulance to the local ER. I convinced her give me an hour to improve. I agreed that if I didn't feel better by then, we could call our doctor. I assured Denise—and myself—that I was OK and that I just needed more rest. More rest would do me good. Not long after Denise left for work, Billy stopped by to check on me. Again, I assured him I was OK and I just needed some more rest. Brandy stopped in to check on me on her way to work. Brandy was worried. She told me that I looked sick and had a grayish color to my skin. Brandy wasn't taking the "I'm OK; I just need rest" bit for an answer. She went to the kitchen and called her mother, explaining to her that I was starting to lose the vibrant color in my face. It was time for Denise to come home. She and Brandy agreed that I needed to go to the hospital. They came in the living room to begin the process of trying to convince me that it was the right thing to do. Denise called Billy to come back over. You simply don't say no when they are all together convincing you that now is the time to go to the hospital; they won the battle. Denise called 911, and we waited for them to arrive.

We came up with a plan. Denise was to come with me in the ambulance, Billy was going to meet us at the hospital, and Brandy was going to make sure everything at home was OK and then come to the hospital as well. We decided that I would get the best care if I went to St. Luke's Allentown campus, which was about twenty miles away. This is where my nightmare began.

A local police officer arrived first. He was asking the questions. Denise was quick to answer because I did not have the energy or inclination to do so. About five to six minutes later, the ambulance arrived, and two EMTs came into the house. One EMT said it would be difficult to get me down the five steps in front of my house. We are remodeling both inside and outside of the house, so our door opens awkwardly onto the porch. The EMT asked if I could walk down. Sure that I could make it, I said, "I think I can." I was wrong. I made it down three steps before I started to hyperventilate, and then I blacked out. The third step was the last thing I remember until I woke up inside the ambulance. There was one thought on my mind at that time: I was trying to tell the EMT I could not breathe. I repeated myself several times, getting more frantic each time. I must have blacked out again.

"We have to go to the closest hospital, or she won't make it," I heard the EMT say. He was talking to the ambulance driver and Denise. I wondered if they were talking about someone else. All right, I would admit it: I was a bit ill and very tired. But I was sure I was not dying. They weren't talking about me. It could not have been me. I was not that sick.

A fraction of a second later, the ceiling of the ambulance had my full attention. It had a shine to it. There was a brilliant light and what I thought was glare from the sun. Did they polish it to get that sheen? I heard the EMT talking. I knew he was speaking, but I wasn't sure whom he was talking to or whom he was talking about. My mind tried sorting out what was happening. And then in a split second, I realized it was me he was talking about. I was the one who might not make it. Hearing those words and knowing they were talking about me was unreal. I was thinking of all the things I did not say to people in my life and all the things left undone. I hoped my family knew how much I love them.

With the urgency of my situation settling in, we were redirected to Blue Mountain Health Systems (old Palmerton Hospital) in Palmerton, Pennsylvania. The hospital is only about six miles from our home. I guess you block things out of your mind when you get that sick or they start meds, because the next thing I heard was scissors. Why would I hear scissors? What would they need scissors for? I found out days later that it was because they had to cut my nightgown and housecoat off me. I opened my eyes long enough to see this large white thing in a man's hand, and he was putting it on my face. I kept trying to back away, but the gurney did not allow much wiggle room. It was going to cover my nose and mouth. I thought he was trying to kill me. Why was he trying to smother me? I could feel my heart beating so fast I thought it was going to jump out of my chest. I could hear my daughter's voice. Why wasn't she trying to stop him? I learned later that no one was trying to kill me. He was trying to help me breathe and keep me alive by placing a mask with some sort of air bag over my mouth and nose. We arrived at Blue Mountain Health System. For a fleeting moment—like a snapshot—I saw people running beside me and possibly one kneeling over or leaning across me.

Chapter 2

Paralyzed by Propofol

Some time had passed. I am not sure how long as I was pretty much out of it. It was like waking up when you are in the half state between sleep and consciousness where the world is calm. I started to hear voices. They were faint and mumbled at first. I remember thinking that my family must be out in the kitchen talking with hushed voices so I could rest. As the voices became clearer, there was an urgency to them. They were short and methodical—not like a discussion, more like rapid-fire responses. Most of the words sounded strange to me. I was unable to glean the meaning of most of them. I heard someone say, "This is minute by minute. For now, let's just keep her alive.

Wide open. Propofol at five titrating to twenty." I became aware that things were moving around. I was trying to place the voices, but none of them sounded familiar to me. It was hard to distinguish just how many there were.

A woman's voice rose above the others. It was more authoritative. Sorting out the meaning of the words seemed impossible. Something about a line, a tube, numbers. I understood "Levaquin." That is an antibiotic. "Propofol." I thought that was the drug Michael Jackson used to sleep. They couldn't be talking about me; if they were giving me Propofol, I would be sleeping. More than anything there was a chorus of beeps and a constant rhythmic humming that I couldn't quite place. I was wondering what was going on, what were these noises, and where were they coming from? Then I heard someone say, "Someone has to go talk to the Smith family." It echoed in my brain: "the Smith family."

What? That was my family. Were they doing all this stuff to me? Where was I? And what the hell were they doing to me? I have never been much for cursing, but my mind was cursing like a sailor on leave. Why was there only darkness? I was asking all of these questions, but no one was answering me. "What is wrong with you people? Why don't you answer me?"

After I asked a few more questions, it hit me: they cannot hear me. I tried opening my eyes, but it was all darkness. I tried to lift up my arm to motion to Denise or the doctor or whoever was attached to the voices I was hearing. My brain was telling my body to get up: "Don't just lie here; swing your legs and move around." But no matter how hard I tried to move my body physically and mentally, my muscles would not move. That is when I realized that I could not move or speak. I could not even open my eyes. Or was there a sheet or something over me? Why couldn't I see? I could hear, and I could feel my heart beating so hard it felt like it would jump out of my chest. Was this what being in a coma felt like? I was nearly exhausted from looking left, then right, then left again—and over and over again. Maybe I would catch a glimpse of something. Maybe someone would notice my eyes moving. They did not.

I didn't know what had happened to me. Why was I in a *coma*? I am saying, "Hello." "Talk to me." "I am right here"—wherever here was. But no one would talk to me. Trying to accept the fact that I couldn't tell anyone how I felt was devastating. I couldn't make eye contact or hand gestures. I was all alone in the darkest corner of the world. Even though I wanted to, I couldn't let anyone in because all I could do was listen to life going on around me— helplessly.

In addition to not being able to move or speak or open my eyes, I believe I lost the ability to smell. I couldn't understand what had happened to my sense of smell. All of the voices were connected to people moving around me, but I smelled no perfume or cologne, no soap or lotion, not even the faint scent of laundry detergent. I should have been able to smell something as close as they were to me. It is surely an odd sensation to have people literally inches from your face and not be able to sense their scent. I should be able to feel their breath. I couldn't even smell that clean hospital smell. At home, it is widely known that I am very sensitive to smell. My family often teases me that I could smell something from miles away. I don't think I realized until now how much the smell of things helps you sort out where you are, who is near you, and what is happening around you. I would have given anything for a familiar smell. I had a sick feeling in the pit of my stomach like a huge brick lodged in my gut. People were all around, busy doing their jobs. My mind was like a runaway train darting from one thought to the other. Was it going to be like this forever? Was there an end? Why was no one explaining to me what was going on? I was alone and so confused. For the first time in my life, I knew what utter loneliness feels like. There was no way to communicate. I was trapped inside my body. This was the worst thing that I had ever experienced.

That was it. I was going to run. I needed to run— run away from this, whatever this was. I was out of there! Everything was dark, but if I could just run, I would end up somewhere. Run. Run. But wait. I still couldn't move.

I wanted to scream, just scream with all my might. I would have thought that being unable to move would feel different—maybe like heaviness or being weighted down. The truth is I didn't feel that. I felt no tingling or numbness—not even pins and needles. Just nothing, like my body was weightless. Except for my lip. I felt a stinging pinch on my bottom lip. I could not feel hot or cold. Typically at home I keep it a very chilly 65 degrees, and I notice any change in temperature—but now nothing.

I thought my hearing was much sharper than before. I could hear conversations close by, even mumblings from further away. Oh, the footsteps! There were soft walkers, stompers—I am sure one had even recently bought new shoes because I could hear them squeak. It was like new gym shoes on a newly waxed basketball court. I heard the rustling of clothing, papers, and perhaps tools that were being pulled from pockets. I honestly thought I could hear people's hearts beating. I could not see, speak, smell, or feel anything, but I sure could hear.

A few moments later, I could hear my son and daughter talking to people whose voices I did not recognize. I thanked God. My kids were here. They would tell someone I was OK and tell me what was going on. So, I started screaming. "Denise, Billy, Brandy, talk to me; please talk to me!" But again, no one would answer me. "Sit up, Sandy. Just sit up, and everyone will know you are alive." But there I lay, waiting in the darkness. Suddenly I felt a burst of energy and tightness in my arms like a sore muscle. I reached up and tried to grab this thing pinching my lip. People were frantically saying, "Don't touch that! Mom, please stop, or they will tie you down." I could hear my son saying I needed to relax and take it easy. My daughter at about the same time was saying, "It is a test; it will be done soon." Why were they yelling at me? I could barely move. What the hell? I was trying to tell someone that this thing in my mouth was cutting my lips and it hurt. Why could I feel my lip and nothing else? What had happened to my body? Why didn't I feel anything else?

I had no sense of time as my thoughts drifted from one topic to another, interrupted by bouts of loud beeps sounding what seemed like impending doom. These were followed almost instantly by someone asking for help or an explanation. These voices came at a higher, more excited pitch. Each time things would seem to settle down, but no help for me ever came. How could they not see what I was going through? Someone asked if I was in pain. I heard my daughter quickly say no. She had just enough medical knowledge to be dangerous, but she was correct. Other than this pinched lip, I felt no pain. I felt a bit calmer with the sound of their voices filling the room. She explained to the other family members in the room that pain has an effect on the body. That if I were in pain, my heart rate, blood pressure, or one of the other monitors would be out of normal range. Well that was interesting because there were moments filled with sheer panic, and I am assuming the monitors did not react. I would have to correct her later.

Wait. I felt something! Brandy was holding my hand and rubbing her thumb up and down my fingers softly. Again I wondered why I could feel my lip and now my hand but no other part of my body. Was I dying? Is this what it felt like to die? I always thought that when you were dying you saw yourself from outside of your body just like in the movies with your spirit hovering near the ceiling in a corner, waiting to get one last look at the world or loved ones. Yet I saw nothing. Brandy made me feel a little bit safer. She was telling me I would be all right. I had the feeling my room was filled with other people, as I could make out bits of conversations. These were mostly stories of the day or about me—the types of discussions families have while all together. I must have drifted off to sleep.

After a little bit, I heard someone say, "How is she?" It might have been my granddaughter Taylor. I heard hushed tones of "Were they in?" "What did they say?" I wondered who exactly were "they." Leaning close to me, I heard "Mem, I just got here." Someone took my hand. It was my grandson Mason.

Someone took my other hand, and then I heard, "It is me. It is Taylor," she said. Mason said, "Taylor and I came as soon as Dad called us." Then I heard another voice. It was Tricia, my son's ex-girlfriend and the mother of Jacob, Taylor, and Mason. Tricia and I get along but really do not visit often and are not very close, since she and my son are no longer an item. When I heard her voice, she was holding my hand and telling me I was going to be OK.

I see Brandy daily, but most of my grandchildren I see monthly. Tricia and I maybe get together twice a year. To know that most of my immediate family was bedside reminded me of when my husband was dying and all the family gathered to say their final good-byes. And how rare was the occasion that Billy and Tricia were in the same room and not annoying each other. Things must have been desperate. That was all I could focus on momentarily. They thought I was dying. They thought I was *dying*.

My family seemed to be rotating their turns talking to me. Each one told me I would be OK. I wanted to yell at ear-piercing decibels, "Do you hear me? Stop telling me I am going to be OK, and tell me what is going on. Please do not count me out yet." I was trying so hard to tell someone that I could hear him or her. I thought I was crying, that someone would hear me, but I was only crying to myself.

Something felt a bit different as I awoke. I could feel my fingers. I was moving my finger! It was still as though my arm and hand were nonexistent, but I was sure I could feel the fabric of the hospital blanket. Why didn't anyone notice that I was moving? Maybe I was not moving.

And then all of a sudden Brandy said, "Mem is moving her fingers." All the grandchildren refer to me as Mem, a nickname for Grandmother. But no one in the room seemed to be thoroughly impressed. Perhaps they were not convinced it was anything but a reflex. To me, I was writing boldly as far as I could reach in the air. "I can hear you and something is hurting my lip," I wrote in the air with my finger. But all Brandy could see was a slight movement of my hand. Billy and Mason continued their conversation over me, literally. Mason was on my left and Billy on my right.

Brandy said, "I think Mem is trying to write or spell out something. She wants to tell us something." Tricia added, "I think Brandy is right. Someone get her a pencil and paper." There is what I can only assume was a search for writing materials. Someone, maybe Tricia, yelled out "Got it!" A pencil was being handed to me. It felt awkward in my hand and it was hard to grip.

I began to write "Help me!" as large as possible. But no one could read what I wrote. If I had not been so scared, it would have been funny listening to them trying to decipher my scratching like the worst game of charades you have ever seen. It was torture listening to them almost figure it out only to go in another direction. There was so much I wanted to write: "I am alive in here. Tell me where I am. Am I dying? Just talk to me." How could they think I was OK? I certainly was not. I was scared and so very tired. At least now they knew I was alive.

Meanwhile they hovered around my bed, each trying to get a glimpse of what I had written. I couldn't understand why they were not reading my note. Why were they acting stupid? It was cruel that they were playing mind games with me.

Document saved and provided by Tricia Seiler

I could hear them consulting with each other about

what the scribbling actually meant. In a consoling tone,

Denise explained to me that they did not understand what

I had written. They each began to yell out answers to the

questions they supposed I was asking. Finally came the

first bits of real information. Where was I? How did I get

there? How long had I been there? They were correct!

Those were the exact questions I needed answers to. I

was alive. I was in the hospital. They were doing some

sort of test. I was so scared that if I could have cried,

shook, and threw up, I would have. The next thing I thought was "Will I ever be me again?" I had so many questions!

Was I dying?

What had happened to me?

Was someone helping me?

When could I go home?

The movement had completely exhausted me. I drifted off to sleep to the sounds of my grandchildren telling me everything was going to be OK and they loved me.

I awoke full of hope. I was rested and raring to go. But I could not fathom what was happening to me now. Everything was black. My eyes defied me. I had no sight. I reached up to motion someone, but my body was useless again. Why did this keep happening? I felt consumed with sadness. One of the worst feelings in the world is when hope is ripped away.

As I awoke this time, I have no idea how long I was asleep. I heard wheels rolling across the floor. A woman was saying we have coffee, tea, and cookies for everyone. Denise was telling Billy to have some coffee. Billy was saying he just had some, but he would have tea. That struck me as odd, as I didn't remember him ever drinking tea. My thoughts twisted and turned as I tried to keep up with all the noise and conversation. I thought it was Tricia who told the kids to have something. I hollered, "No! They only bring that cart when someone is dying. I can still hear you. Take the goddamned cookies and coffee away. I am still alive. You have the wrong room." But everyone kept eating and drinking. I was so upset I felt sick. Once again, I thought I should run—get out of there. I was running and running, but I was really still lying motionless in the bed, again not being able to move a muscle. I don't know exactly how to describe it other than saying I was screaming, yelling, crying, and sick to my stomach. My heart was beating out of my chest and shaking in the dark. I began to have a hard time focusing. I was avoiding sleep with all my might, as I was not sure what would happen if I gave in to it. I struggled to keep my mind active thinking about my life, their lives, and the things I said or did not say. Finally, the meds must have taken over, and I was out cold again.

My life became rounds of sleep followed by waking just to come to grips again with my situation. Each time I awoke, I forget that I was trapped inside a motionless body in a vicious unending cycle. I was sure I could hear part of a sentence before I drifted off only to wake up to the ending of another. This added to my confusion and made no sense to me. I think it made me more afraid. It was hard to concentrate and try to sort out the words and what I thought were medical terms.

When the noises got low and there was nothing to listen to but the hum of machines, my mind would wander. I tried to control my thinking and focus on being at home. I tried to remember every detail of my living room with me sitting in my recliner, holding my cat, and feeling the warmth of him and the Tweety throw blanket on my lap. I tried to recall the low sound of the Lifetime movie network on my TV. Sometimes I would try to imagine myself somewhere else—a nice restaurant or a shopping outing. Unfortunately, I was unable to keep my mind from going to the dark side.

Chapter 3

The Darkness

My mind would turn suddenly and unexpectedly like the violent wind of a summer storm whipping me to the darkest recesses. Thoughts of my death slipped in quickly. I guess I had watched one too many episodes of shows involving medical examiners because I found myself thinking not only of my death but the aftermath. There would be an autopsy to find the cause of the death. At first, I imagined huge white, fluffy sheep and counting them as they jumped over the picket fence. It was not enough to stop the thoughts of death. Again, I was brought back to the thoughts of scalpels cutting my flesh, the buzz of a saw cutting through the bones in my chest, and a crunching sound as the examiner pulled the bones apart to access my insides. Oh God, would I be able to feel it? What if it was just like at that moment, and I could hear what they were doing? At what point would I actually die? When they began to remove my organs? Would the doctor be able to tell my heart was still beating? Would they put me back together with a staple gun? Just as in a horror movie, ominous music overwhelmed me, slow at first and gradually increasing as the danger neared. Then came the voices of family discussing visiting schedules, the doling out of chores, and things that needed to be done at home as life went on around me. I heard what I thought were shopping carts and small groups of people almost out of earshot. I could not make out their exact words, but the tempo of their words gave me something to concentrate on for the moment.

Trying to change my internal monologue was a constant battle, a true test of will between two sides of my mind. I pleaded for something else to focus on: a new noise or new voice, anything to distract me from these horrible thoughts. The harder I tried to change the thought pattern, the more difficult it seemed to do just that. Would they drain my blood? Would that be the final sound I heard, my own blood dripping out in a large metal industrial sink? I preferred the last thing I heard to be the voices of my family, a room filled with love and laughter.

Why is it that my thoughts were not filled with unicorns, rainbows, or kittens and puppies rolling around in green grass under beams of sunshine? How could I keep these things in the forefront of my mind?

When I woke again, it was quiet but I could hear things in the distance. Without a close distraction, my mind jumped from place to place again. And the darkness entered. Since I was in the hospital apparently getting treatment, they must have already known what was wrong with me. What if they did not do an autopsy? I feared they would pull that sheet over me and wheel me down to the human storage cooler with its large metal drawers. Then I would be in a box—I am claustrophobic—and then in a coffin in the ground. Dear God, please don't let me suffocate to death in my coffin. In an effort to force out these thoughts, I began to hum. It was the first music that popped in my head. It was unrecognizable at first but the tune came easily to me. Then I burst into the lyrics: "The devil went down to Georgia; he was looking for a soul to steal." It did not bother me that I did not know all the words to the verse; I knew the chorus, so I kept singing! I sang it over and over again.

It did not stop the darkness from creeping back in. It was like a thick fog at dusk, and there was nothing I could do to stop it. The devil. Hell. Was I in hell then? It seemed logical that this was a torture technique. I may very well have been losing my mind because now I saw a large group of people that I had never seen before. I believed the strangers were just there to watch me. The faces were expressionless. All wore dark clothing and had stiff body language. Why were they staring at me? I looked around the room; it almost appeared to be a museum, a large open expanse with a spotlight highlighting me in a glass display box. I reached up and pushed on the thick glass top, but it would not move. I looked like a mime in the imaginary box, testing each side for a way out. There did not appear to be one. I started yelling to the viewers to let me out. "Help me!" They did not respond—not even eye contact. I was now banging on the glass; perhaps I could just crack it. The stark figures seemed to be gathering in small groups. There were smiling and nodding with casual glances in my direction like a viewing party for my suffering. I kicked the bottom with my bare feet and wedged my body to get as much leverage as I could to pop one of the glass panels out of place. Fists flailing, I pounded with as much strength as I could muster, but still there was no response from the gallery. I was crying now with each blow because my knuckles were sore and bloody. Why did they refuse to help me? I was so exhausted, I could no longer fight.

I had just enough time to catch my breath before I was tossed back into thoughts of my death—images of me in my coffin surrounded by satin-white quilting gathered with small pearl buttons. It appeared pristine. Then flashed pictures of small insects entering from a small crack in the seam. The insects marched toward me like little brownish-red armored soldiers making steady pace toward my pure-white blanket. The first one breached the blanket and touched my skin, and every hair on my body stood straight up. They crawled all over my body, relentlessly biting and gnawing on my skin, the little hard-bodied devils swarming to attack. I was frozen inside my body, unable to swipe them off as they devoured me. The sound of their feasting caused sheer panic. The smell of freshly dug dirt and blood now filled the space as blood began to soak through the satin blanket. There was a thick tightness to the air, which had become almost humid. It grew harder to breathe with every passing moment.

"Three little fishes in an itty-bitty pool. Three little fishes and a mommy fishy too." What was the next line? I remember singing this song to my children hundreds of times. I tried again now. "Three little fishes in an itty-bitty pool. Three little fishes and a mommy fishy too." Nope, blank again. But I could see the little fish swimming playfully in the pool with its calm blue water. Wait, there were bubbles behind the fish. I could not see what was in the water, but the bubbles were getting closer to them. Ripples in the water grew to a swoosh as it closed in on the fish. Something was after them. I wanted to save them, but I could not. I was the momma fish treading water against the strong current, helpless as the swirling water and bubbles overtook them. I needed to think of something else. "Mind, please go somewhere else," I pleaded.

"R-E-S-P-E-C-T, find out what it means to me," I sang as loud as I could to try to delay the next thought. I saw myself in a wooden coffin with no frills, a plain pine box. I felt a single drop of water drip on my face. I wanted to wipe it from my cheek, but I still could not move. It felt cool and dare I say almost refreshing because the summer heat felt trapped in the box with me. A steady pace of little drips began. As the drops become larger and more powerful, the bits of water splashed across my face. The drips progressed to what was now a steady stream of water pouring in. I wanted to turn my head away. If only I could reach up and plug up the hole! I felt the water pooling, filling the spaces between my body and the box. It was getting harder to breathe. The water was claiming space where precious air belonged. I knew screaming was a futile waste of energy because no one could hear me. I started to cry because that was all I could do. My salty tears added to the depth of the water. I was going to drown. The water had risen by now and was covering nearly all of me. I wanted to tilt my head back to keep my face as close to the now-small pocket of air near the top of my coffin, but I was still a statue. I took a breath, and this time it was filled with moisture, causing me to cough. I began gasping, but it was no use. I was about to take my final breath.

But then a momentary reprieve from those horrifying thoughts brought relief. A very cheery man told me good morning and that it was time we started our day together. I was not sure who he was, but his voice sounded happy. He was going to be with me for a while, and we had much to do. "Got to love this guy," I thought, since I was sure he knew I would not be of much help to him. He explained that things were not quite the way he liked and we had some organizing to do. I knew he was busy because I could hear packages being opened and fingers banging on computer keys. It reminded me of potato-chip bags being opened. Although I was sure potato chips weren't being opened, I was curious about the packages' contents.

My time was spent hearing someone talk, or I was sleeping or just lying there waiting for someone to talk to me. It was dark, pitch black. It seemed like forever, but I could still not open my eyes, so I had no idea what time it was. Then there was a new voice—a man's. He was telling me, "Don't breathe, Mrs. Smith, don't breathe. Just relax." I could hear my son saying, "Mom, please relax." My daughter then said, "Mom, if you don't relax they are going to strap you down." Billy was emphatically saying, "Relax." Then Brandy said, "Mem, you are going to be OK. Just settle down."

"Oh my God!" I thought. "I am moving. Why do they want me to stop breathing? Do they want me to give up? I am not ready to give up. That made me more determined to fight. I will show them. Can someone tell them that, please?"

I honestly do not know which is worse, the not knowing where I was or the fear of knowing I was in the hospital and thinking I was dying. No matter what they said, I could not relax. I needed to move as much as I could, so they knew I was in here fighting. I knew my body was moving because of their constant pleas for me to stop. I was not sure I was controlling the movements. But it didn't matter to me as long as I did not go back to how I'd been before—motionless.

Faintly I thought I could hear Denise's voice asking why we were not going on Route 248. Someone explained to her that we were taking the bridge to jump on the turnpike. I started to wonder what bridge they were talking about. There was a bridge by my house, but that was not near the turnpike. Was I being moved?

A new voice broke the silence in my room. Would this person notice that I was in here? I was not sure how much longer I could bear to be trapped in there, longing for something external to keep my attention. I couldn't feel the position of my body. Was I lying down, sitting, or hanging from the ceiling? It was so odd not to be able to feel the positioning of my body. I guess it really did not matter, but thinking about it occupied my time. The beeps and buzzes didn't bother me as much. The same footsteps repeated over and over. It made me want to yell, "Who are you?" Again, either I passed out, went to sleep, or the drugs took over.

Waking up, I asked myself, "Why am I being tortured? What did I ever do that was so horrible that God is punishing me?" I didn't cheat or steal. I never killed anyone. I did take the Lord's name in vain often, but this punishment did not fit the crime. Was God torturing me, or was I doing this to myself? I could barely think straight at that point. If only I could pinch myself and wake up. What if I never woke up? I was ready to deal. I promised to continue to be a good person, not a better person. I would not take anything for granted. I would enjoy every sunrise and flower. I would not be stingy with my feelings. I would help mankind.

I did not know exactly where I was, but now it was different than before. I felt it. I don't remember motion. The voices seemed to have changed. I just heard someone ask for a scalpel, A-line, central line, and blood gases. A scalpel? Was someone operating on me? Was this going to save me? When all you can do is hear, your brain can really take what you are hearing and distort it. I thought I was having a big operation, but it was just a small cut in my neck. This place felt emptier. Was I alone? No. Someone was explaining that there were no chairs in this room because they wanted the patient to be totally accessible. The nurse was giving the lowdown, and I was starting to feel like I knew a bit more even though I could

tell the directions were not directed at me. She explained

that a MICU nurse or nurses would be with me all the

time. I knew someone was there—or many someones.

Once again I woke up not being able to see but hearing

voices that I didn't recognize, and it sent chills up my

spine. When that happened, I thought the little hairs on

my neck would stand up. But this was different. There was

not much noise, only muted voices and the squeaky sound

that rubber shoes make on the floor. I had the oddest

feeling that someone was intermittently staring at me, but

the constant darkness remained. If they were working on

me, I could not tell because I still could not feel my body. I

lay there just listening to the sounds, guessing what each

one might be. This seemed to work as a coping technique,

helping me be less scared.

I heard a somewhat eerie sound. It took me a bit to

remember. I knew that sound. It was a sliding door. Why I

had a sliding door instead of a regular door was a mystery. The sound meant someone came in. The someone was humming—not a peppy tune exactly but more calming like a lullaby. I wanted to say, "I know you're here." But I couldn't. There was the sound again. They left and I was alone again.

I wondered if my family looked at me like I was the shell of a person just lying here. I felt like a pair of ears and a brain. I hoped against hope they could see me inside here. "Please discover I'm still alive and inside here. Please say it out loud." I needed someone to say the words. This waiting and loneliness was nearly intolerable. I was drowning in fear with no end in sight. Please save me from the darkness. I was petrified to think about what would come next. Could it be worse?

Chapter 4

The Light

Then mercifully there was a break to the bleakness. I could see a light. For a fleeting moment I wondered, "Is this it? Is this the light at the end of the tunnel?" Somehow I thought it would feel warm and comforting, but this was stark and cold. Why was someone shining a small bright light in my eye? I could hear my daughter questioning the person, "Why is one pupil different than the other? Is she aware of what is going on?" The person responded, "It will help if you talk to her." I wanted to say it would help if they all would listen to me! I could hear in Denise's voice that she was stressed but as usual trying to keep everyone else in control. She is that type. As long as she is getting information and can feel that she can control even the minutest thing, she feels solace.

Then I heard Billy III, Billy's oldest son. He stood next to me. His words were hopeful, as were everyone's. I was going to be OK. But the words did not match the tremors in their voices. To me it sounded like fear. Billy III brought his new girlfriend. Everyone sounded glad to meet her. I was thinking, "Come on, kid. You know I hate people seeing me without my hair done!" Now there were two more people I hoped would notice I was in there. Maybe I could get their attention. I felt like I had repeated these pleas a thousand times in hopes that it would make them come true.

I could hear Denise telling them, "They are going to let us know if anything changes." What did that mean? I hoped it did not mean if I got worse. Honestly, how could this get any worse? Thoughts swirled in my head like a tornado. I began to question whether or not I really wanted to know what was happening to me. Would it terrify me further? Should I try to ignore them? Hell, that was a good question. I couldn't make a choice. The choice was made for me because I had no way of plugging up my ears. And truthfully, I was so desperate for someone to find me in there that if I could, I would have gotten down on my knees and begged for help.

In my mind, I was screaming. If I was dying, why were they all telling me I was going to be OK? There was almost no silence in my mind. I could hear a chorus of random beeps and bongs followed by slight buzzing sounds. Each series of these sounds in the darkness brought a new fear. I knew I was in the hospital. I hoped I was at St. Luke's. I wondered, if I was in Allentown, what floor was I on? What room was I in? I guessed it did not really matter, as I had no control anyway.

My kids had been here for what seemed like a long while. Their discussion was about the cold weather. I would have loved to feel the cold right then. Billy was looking for someone to make a cafeteria run with him during quiet time. I wasn't sure how often quiet time came or how long it lasted, but to me it came quickly and lasted a long time.

It seemed strange to recognize people by their sounds. To keep from going insane, I tried to listen for the same sounds more than once. Then I gave them names so they did not seem so scary. These names included Squeaky Shoes, Tick Tock, Jingles, and Soft Walker. It helped break up the mind-bending silence. "Squeaky Shoes, I know you were here before," I thought. "I can also tell by the way you seem to jump up on the rolling chair rather than sit very quietly. Not being able to see or know your name, I will call you Squeaky Shoes. I enjoy when you are here, as you bring much-needed distraction. I listen to you going near and far. Sometimes I hear you in the hall with maybe four or five other sets of shoes." There was always lively conversation, but I couldn't accurately make out all the words. I was becoming familiar with those around me.

Some people walked with more of a stride to their step, as though half-running. Others were full-on running. Still others walked so slowly but with a little thump when their feet hit the floor. There were a few that walked so softly I did not know they were near me until the swooshing sound of their clothing was near me or they started typing. Sometimes I thought people came in and out of the room without me knowing. Every so often, I could recognize the click of high heels on the tile floor.

I kept listening. Twice I thought I heard the same person only because when they got close I could hear the tick-tick-tick very faintly. I think it was a watch. I imagined Tick Tock was old school with a classic-style watch—no digital display for him. I looked forward to Jingles. Jingles liked charms on a bracelet or chain, or it was small change in a pocket.

As hard as I tried, I could not sort out the pattern of visitors. There seemed to be a steady flow with long periods of silence. I wished the radio was playing. Most of the time, I enjoyed listening to Billy socializing with what I presumed were my nurses or other hospital staff. He was generally a pacer, but I had not detected too much of that; maybe the room was too small for a good lap around. The conversations between my family were varied. Sometimes my daughter filled the silence by reading out loud. I listened for the spark of clarity as though she might relay some important personal information about my situation, my cat, etc. But it seemed she was just filling the void. Brandy spoke to me with gentleness in her voice. I knew they must all be worried beyond belief. I often recognized periods of uncomfortable silence between my family members. Even though I was sure they did not know I

could hear, they seemed to be editing themselves. I
guessed negative words had been banned from my room.

Sometimes in these horrible days, I saw my
husband. I was just so sleepy I could not fight to stay
awake one second longer, and I allowed myself to drift to
sleep. Or I thought it was sleep, reaching the point where
I had no fight left in me. The blackness shifted. All I saw
was gray with black shadows on the right side and in front.
There was a soft light illuminating from the rear and to the
left. Bill, my husband, was standing halfway back. He had
one arm outstretched with his hand out. He looked young
with his dark-brown hair swooped up in a pompadour style
right down to the little bump on his nose, a remnant of a
break he refused to have fixed. It was as if no time had
passed for us. That feeling of home flooded me. He was
telling me to go back. "Go back. You are not done yet," he
said. Oddly I felt calm in those moments.

At first, I thought he had come to keep me safe. But he only said those words. Yes, I am positive it was my husband because he never talked a lot. He always got right to the point. I tried to explain to him that I didn't know where I was, but they were telling me not to breathe, and he was telling me to go back. I was not sure what I was supposed to do. Maybe seeing him gave me the strength and determination I needed.

Suddenly a loud noise drew my attention from him. I was back. Back from where I do not exactly know. But my husband and the calmness I had felt were gone, and the blackness and noise had returned. Later I found out they were telling me not to struggle to breathe because I was trying to breathe against the ventilator. One is telling me not to breathe; my husband is telling me go back. But go back where? What was happening to me? If someone didn't tell me soon, I would go crazy. I do not dare think what would have become of me without that boost of gumption.

In the darkness I could hear things being moved around me, papers rustling, muddled voices, and the sound of beeps, bongs, and various warnings from machines, but everything was just black. Outside my door I could hear three people talking about a woman who had just passed away from the flu. I was not sure about the relationship to the woman, but the sobs told me she was loved.

It seemed to me my children and Brandy were there most of the time. Denise must have had a hard time with the silence because she was reading again. I thought it was the morning newspaper and Facebook. Brandy told me about her boyfriend, Dustin, and his well wishes and shared a story about Miss Kitty, her cat. Billy told me about those around me and stories about goings on at home. I didn't think they realized I hung on their every word, but it brought me comfort either way. Quite often I heard someone asking, "How is our patient today?" This was always followed by "She is doing OK." I knew when they were getting ready to leave. They came much closer, and I always had a moment of hopefulness that when they leaned in to kiss me good night or good-bye, they would notice me in there.

Thoughts keep running through my mind. I noticed that I was not eating or drinking. If I was alive, what was I living on? Why didn't I need food? I did not even feel hungry. Now that I think about it, I do not remember drinking anything either. The medications I took on a regular basis caused me to have dry mouth, so I always had a drink with me, sometimes two. But now I didn't even feel thirsty at all. Did this confirm I was dying?

How long had I been like this? There were many times I started to think about what was happening to me, and I just froze. I couldn't face it. Then I heard someone talking to me about the weather, what we had planned for the day, or just saying good morning. It made me feel safer when the nurses acknowledged me. I tried to avoid sleep because I knew when I woke up there would be those moments of panic where I could not remember what happened or where I was. Each time I woke, I wondered if I had been sleeping for moments, hours, or days. The movie *Groundhog Day* came to mind as I awoke having to come to the realization yet again that I was hopelessly trapped in there.

For the next few days, I was in and out. My mind was fuzzy. Maybe foggy is a better description. I didn't hear much more than footsteps and mumbling. I could hear a woman explaining to someone unidentified that we were going to try cutting back on something. I wasn't sure what it was or what it was doing for me. Was that the thing keeping me in this state or the thing keeping me alive?

All at once someone was shining a light in my eye again and telling me to wake up. Was I still paralyzed? Why did she have to hold my eyelid open? Did any part of my body work? Oh, my God. She was talking to me. She knew I was alive. She was trying to help me. She took away the darkness. I still could not move or talk, but I could see. I was so happy I could feel tears welling up in my eyes.

The room was flooded with a bright white light. It was so bright that by instinct I wanted to look away and my eyelids wanted to flinch. It took a moment for me to focus. As the bright beam of light dimmed, things started to come into focus. Everything in the room was so beautiful. I wanted to look at everything: the light coming in the window, even the machines. I opened and closed my eyes several times, each time wondering if it would all disappear again. I was crying again, but this time because I could see. There it was. The familiar white board with the

St. Luke's logo, there to document the day, the changing of the guards so to speak, including nurse, doctor, tech staff, even the cleaning person. I looked around at faces I did not recognize, but I could see something in their eyes. Maybe this was relief because that is what I was feeling.

I started to feel a bit of a sensation in my fingertips and toes, a tingle that was spreading. It was not painful and not as strong a feeling as pins and needles. I was filled with anticipation at the prospect of being able to move. Now I only hoped my expectations became reality. Focusing in like a laser on my toes, I prayed, "Come on, little guys, just move a bit." And they moved! It was thrilling to just wiggle my toes. Wait until my family could see this! I was overwhelmed with gratitude that I would be able to again see the faces of my children and grandchildren, my house, and even my cat too.

Just then I realized what was in my mouth was a tube of a ventilator. My first thought was "Will I be on this machine forever?" I began to feel this uncomfortable feeling: fluids dripping from my mouth, the ache of my jaw being open for such a long time, and the pinching in my lip.

I believe it was the fourth day into my MICU stay when the doctor asked me if I wanted the tube out. I could not speak, but in my mind, I was yelling "Hell yes! Please get it out." Within a minute, he had it out. I had never thought anything could be so fast. He held the tube in my mouth, and in one fell swoop it was out. A nurse stood next to him with a trash bin to catch it and whisk it away. It was so fast I didn't even feel a thing. I thought there would be pain, but there was none. Shortly after that, I could talk. I could feel my legs and hands again. It was true. I was getting better.

I still had lots of things hooked up to me, including a tube in my neck. I was not exactly sure what they all did. Still I was so happy to be alive and getting better, I did not care what I was hooked to. Around this time I found out that it had indeed been a ventilator down my throat along with an IV in my wrist, another in my arm, a tube in my nose, and a shunt in my neck with stitches to keep it in place. For the rest of the day, they slowly removed things from me until I was down to the IV and a tube in my neck where they put medication. I was filled with hope that I would recover, hope that I would go home. But when the doctor came, guess what? He had a mask on. He said the test came back positive. I was unaware of a test. I had the flu. So everyone coming in my room had to wear a mask. They also had to get a flu shot if they had not already had one.

What put me in the hospital was exacerbation of my COPD, the flu, pneumonia, and the broken-heart syndrome Takotsubo cardiomyopathy, which happens almost exclusively to women. It causes the heart to become misshapen to resemble an octopus trap. With all this I now understand why I was so weak and tired. They told me my body went into total traumatic shock because it could not handle being so sick. That afternoon my grandson, Jake, came to see me. Later that day Billy III came and even my niece Stacy. All these days my daughter, son, and granddaughter, Brandy, sat with me, only leaving my side when forced to by the quiet hour at the MICU. Way back in my mind, I knew they were there even when they were not speaking. They were there to make sure I was taken care of. Thinking of them being there made me feel safe. Later that night I was taken out of MICU and moved to a regular room. Two days later, very weak but very much alive, we were getting ready to go home. I was still so weak that I could not take two steps by myself.

Chapter 5

The Return Home

❧

Once I returned home, one of the first visitors I had brought me a welcome-home gift: a tray of cookies. As we sat drinking coffee, it struck me as odd that the refreshments to celebrate my homecoming were identical to the ones offered to comfort my family in the hospital. I have to admit, it freaked me out.

I slept on the recliner in my living room for nearly two weeks. Denise or Brandy slept over on my sofa every night. I could not walk to the bathroom, use the commode, or get a drink, and I could barely even stand up on my own. Thank God they were there because I could not do anything alone. Honestly even if I had been more mobile, I felt like I needed someone near me so I would not feel alone. As I sat on my chair, my body so exhausted, I began to drift off to sleep, and the feeling rushed back to me. My body jolted; sometimes I thought it was my brain just making sure my limbs could move. I was sent home with both a visiting nurse and a home health aide. Little things caused so much anxiety. From the weather alert on a cell phone to the reminder beeps on the microwave, sounds took me right back to lying paralyzed. During Nurse Brenda's first visit, she removed the stitches from my neck. In my opinion, Brenda is one of the nicest people I know. She is the kind of nurse that you can tell really cares about her patients. It was not just a job to her. She went above and beyond. Amy, my home health aide, was there to help me take a shower, wash my hair, and even fix a bed.

At first, I was a bit embarrassed by the loss of modesty. I did feel a loss of pride at not being able to do simple daily tasks. Amy showed me much respect, and I knew it was time to swallow my pride and allow her to help me. She made it easy for me to adjust.

I did not tell anyone about what was bothering me. I thought no one would believe me or they would think I was crazy. I slowly started telling Denise bits of my memories. One day I told her I thought I heard someone offering them coffee and cookies. She confirmed that did happen, looking at me like she was stunned. Over the next week, I ended up telling Denise more of the things I could remember. I was relieved when she told me the things I remembered did actually happen.

The more we spoke and compared accounts of the event, the more we found more common points. It seemed to shock her more every day that I could recall details of things that happened and the conversations they had in my presence. I eventually opened up and told her everything I was feeling.

In sharing tales of our experiences, I heard about the first moments when my lung doctor came to the waiting room to speak to my family, having to tell them that I might not pull through. I could picture Denise standing there taking each bit of information in. Billy was probably taking short steps back and forth, listening to what was said. Brandy—well she is a bit sassy in these situations. I could see her being impatient, not wanting anyone to hem and haw around, and thinking, "Let us back to see my grandmother already" so she could judge for herself. She is protective that way. And I could see Billy III sitting, just analyzing the situation.

I also found out that it is rare that someone can hear or feel what is going on with such clarity. If I ever get put to sleep again, this could or may never happen again.

After about two weeks, I could manage on my own a bit better and started sleeping in my own bed. You would think now that I was getting better, this would be the end of my story. But it was not over yet.

It was about the end of March when Denise and Brandy began to worry that I couldn't sleep more than about four hours a night. I was having horrific nightmares. Brandy bought me a journal and said it might help me to jot down whatever I could remember about the dreams in the book. I diligently began to notate my dreams along with bits and pieces of conversations I heard. By the end of March, one night I sat up in bed at about 3:30 a.m. I had had a nightmare. My dreams seemed to be feeling more and more real. In this dream, there was a hand coming at me, holding something white. I was pushing my head back in the pillow, but he kept coming. He was going to kill me. I was screaming, "Why? Please don't smother me!" I didn't know who it was, nor did I care. Even though it was just a hand, I knew it was a man. Then I awoke.

Looking around I knew I was in my bedroom and safe. I

didn't feel safe, but after a few moments I stopped

shaking. It took another two hours to get back to sleep.

Sometimes I woke up to footsteps, machines running, or

the sense of things being moved around me—not real

scary, but I still had to sit up, look around, and get my

bearings because I did not know initially if it was real or

not.

Reoccurring was the feeling of total isolation in my

dreams. I would be released from the hospital to come

home in the paralyzed and blind state, set up in a hospital

bed in the living room with family and friends dropping by

for momentary visits. I'd spend hours upon hours in

darkness, confined to my bed, reduced to little more than

some accessory houseplant that needed occasional

tending. I experienced the ache I felt at not being able to

ever say the things I could have said, not being able to tell them I loved them. Years would go by not being able to see my grandchildren and great grandchildren grow up and begin their lives, wondering if they would ever figure out that I could hear them, so desperate for just one more conversation no matter what the topic. I presumed that eventually the visits would taper off as everyone's lives got back to the normal rhythm of daily tasks. How would I cope with the loneliness? This would be no way to live, just lying there, wasting away.

The next night I woke up about 2:00 a.m. so scared I could not get back to sleep. I didn't really know what woke me up, so I just lay in bed, still afraid to close my eyes. For the next two or three nights, I had no dreams, and I thought and hoped it was over. I don't know the time, but the next night, I woke up crying, sweating, and shaking with a pounding heart. For some reason, my brain put two things together. Someone with something white on his hand had been trying to smother me. I called out to them as loud as I could. But still no one helped me. Then I

realized I was at home alone, and this was yet another

nightmare. There were so many nightmares.

A few nights later, I was jolted awake at 4:00 a.m.

in terror. Somehow I had been lying in a field of tall

grasses. The night air was crisp, and I felt chilled, wearing

only a hospital gown. The sky was lit with the glow of a

thousand stars. Although I could not move, it was

peaceful. A slight breeze made the grasses sway gently. A

feeling of being pursued overwhelmed me, and then I

heard it—the crunching sound of stalks being flattened as

someone was creeping toward me. Out of the corner of my

eye, I noticed the landscape changing as the thicket

cleared a few inches at time. My attention was quickly

drawn lower to the ground, and instead of seeing a

person, I saw a mangy four-legged animal. The wolflike

animal was quiet until now, but making eye contact

changed that. It began to snarl, and I was speechless with fear.

It leaned back on its hind legs and let out a tremendous howl. Suddenly another creature emerged from the grassland. They began to circle, breathing deeply, almost snorting. Hackles up, the first one chomped on my gown and pulled. A large swatch remained in his jowls, and this seemed to incite them. I started to holler, hoping to scare them. While they stepped back temporarily, they quickly discerned that I was no physical threat. I knew I had been bitten, but I felt no pain. My view of the sky changed as the team began to yank at my lifeless limbs. The tugging continued in spite of my gut-wrenching noises. In concert now, the two began to drag me through the field. The beasts flipped my body, and my face dragged on the rough and bumpy ground at a pace that became nearly a frenzy. Then next second I awoke to flailing my arms in my bed, sweating and hyperventilating.

I thought maybe the whole experience of being paralyzed and unable to communicate was a dream. I sat up for a few minutes before I got out of bed to see if there was really a commode and walker in my house. Yes, they were both there—plus a breathing machine, a whole lot of meds, and discharge papers from the hospital. It was no dream; it really did happen.

This time I sat up in bed. I was terrified by the latest nightmare. I felt like I had been tortured. Every muscle in my body held the tension that sometimes follows extreme pain. I shivered as I recollected each surge of voltage as it found a path through me. It was like shock treatments on the only part of me that was still working— my brain. A loud car passed on the street outside my house, and the lights made a familiar shadow on my bedroom wall. I understand now that it might have been a dream. I struggle sometimes to tell the difference in those first moments when I wake. Oftentimes I'm pleading, "If this is a dream, please someone wake me up." This is not how I imagined I would be spending my golden years, waking up sweating and scared of someone trying to kill me night after night.

I opened my eyes to a sunny beautiful day, and I felt good. It is a bit curious that it was 8:00 a.m. and no one woke me up. So, I got out of bed and, using my walker, moseyed down the hall to the living room. I was alone and the TV was off. This was odd, as someone had always been there quite early to make coffee and watch the news. I picked up my cell and called my son, but there was no answer. I tried my daughter and then my granddaughter, Brandy. Both went directly to voicemail. I kept trying to call them all again and again. I was really starting to worry. What if I needed help and no one was around to help me? I was not strong enough yet to do too much for myself. What if something happened to one of them and they didn't want to tell me? What if something horrible happened to all of them?

I maneuvered my walker so that I could get closer to the window on the other side of the room. It is a huge window that overlooks my front porch and the street. The sun was pouring in, but the street was empty. No people, no cars, no animals or even birds. I live in a small town, and we are a close community. I can usually see at least a neighbor walking a dog or a child heading to school. I was starting to really feel uneasy, even a little angry. They all knew I did not like to be left on my own right now. Why were they doing this to me? When they got there, I was going to give them a piece of my mind for sure. I headed to the front door, only a few steps from the window. For some reason I was unable to open the door. I could turn the handle, but the door would not budge.

Starting to panic a bit now, I decided to try the back door. It was on the other side of the kitchen. I didn't have enough strength, so the best option was to sit on my walker and push myself using both my feet and arms. The walker moved a little more smoothly on the tile of kitchen floor versus the thicker living room carpeting. I could get to the refrigerator, but then the pathway was too tight for the walker. I had to rest a bit before walking those final few steps.

One more attempt to each of their cell phones produced no response. "OK. Here I go. Up and a few steps to find them!" I made it. The back door has no window, so there was nothing to see. But this door would not open either. Try as I might, I was stuck and all alone. Just as I began banging on the door, I sat up in my bed.

Why were these nightmares so realistic?

At times I found myself lying in bed staring at the large red numbers of a digital clock, waiting for a sign that says, "You are home. It is OK." Then Pudders would bound in. He liked to eat first thing in the morning. So, if I was not up and moving by 6:30 a.m., he was meowing, letting me know it was OK to get up.

I slept OK for two nights after that waking-up nightmare. Then came the dream that scared me the most. I sat up around midnight, shocked because this nightmare was so real. I could see myself lying on a hard, shiny table, covered with a sheet. My family was all in the room. I could hear them. Someone was handing out milk, coffee, tea, and cookies. They were telling stories about me, stories about things I did to them or with them while they were growing up. They were laughing and crying at the same time. People, people, people! I was under the sheet. Was I dead? I couldn't be, I thought, my mind still racing. Is your mind the last thing to shut down before you die? I felt like my body was shaking so bad the table must have been moving. I was alive under there. What was wrong with everyone? "Please look at me!" All I could think was that it didn't matter why I was there. I was alive, so I should not be there. I was screaming, "Stop!" But they simply ignored me. Each person in his or her scrubs and masks simply prepared for some surgical procedure. I wanted to sit up and grab the scalpel.

Then I realized I was at home in my bed. It was another nightmare. I spent the rest of the night awake, watching *King of Queens*.

At that time I was having a nightmare about twice a week. It was like someone playing a horror movie over and over for me. I didn't care how many times I told myself they were dreams. I had a very hard time believing they were dreams. They were so vivid. I sat and went over them again and again in my mind, trying to make sense of each one. How anyone could keep going through this was astonishing. I was never sure if it was a nightmare or if I was back in the middle of the torment. I was not sure how much longer I could stand this without losing my mind.

I flashed ahead to the funeral home. My family passed before my coffin in their mourning attire with pale, tear-stained faces, one by one in succession. Each one placed some small token or ornament inside my coffin. Again, I screamed, trying to get just one of them to spot the glimmer of life in my eyes. As the line of people ended, one shadowy figure appeared, and he tucked in the fabric and flowers that lay strewn about. Slowly the lid squashed out the daylight. I knew they were moving me. I clawed and banged desperately, trying to escape. But just as before, I went unnoticed.

I lay still, having spent every last drop of energy I had on the failed attempts for rescue. What was that sound? It could not be, but it was. It was the sound of dirt. What may have been handfuls at first increased to shovelfuls. There was no more hope. Was I damned to spend eternity alone in this forsaken place?

At about 5:00 a.m. I woke up shaking with a sick feeling in the pit of my stomach. I was sure I could hear the footsteps of someone walking down the hall to my room, slowly approaching my bed and leaning over me. The background noise was filled with people crying. I felt like he was reaching out to touch me. My cat meowed, and I sat up as quickly as my body allowed. I needed to get out of this room and head to the kitchen. I had no idea why I felt like that. My son was in the kitchen making coffee. He talked to me until I felt calmer.

Another night, another nightmare sent a shiver down my spine. I could hear a beep and could sense someone standing beside me. I could even hear this person breathing in and out, in and out. I could feel my heart beating in my chest. I was so scared I don't think I could have screamed even if I could have spoken. I had the eerie feeling of not knowing if this person was there to help me or hurt me. It was the horrible feeling of not knowing what was going on. If only I could have seen or felt. But all I could do was lie there in the darkness alone. All of a sudden, I opened my eyes, and, yes, it was another nightmare. I still shake because it seemed so real.

The nightmares are lessening, but there are many nights I can't sleep. I don't know why I can't sleep. I even take a sleeping pill. I really do think that in the back of my mind, there is something that happened that I can't remember. And that memory will not let me sleep. I still need someone to talk to. Denise found me a professional to talk to. Her name is Candice. She gives me hope because she believes we can work on coping skills to help me overcome the extreme anxiety I feel. Physically, I am still so tired. I can only do a few dishes at a time.

I just want people to know my story. It is true, so if something like this happens to you, you are not crazy. Some people can hear or feel after everyone thinks they are under anesthesia. I don't want anyone to think the hospital stay was bad. Everyone from doctor to cleaning staff was helpful and professional. As for my health, I am still weak, and things take me a bit longer, but I am getting around better. The heart doctor at my follow-up visit told us my heart went back to its normal size and shape after about three months, and I can walk about fifteen feet by myself. I also go out to eat and shop. I use a wheelchair, but I go!

I think as the months go by, I will continue to heal. I had a bit of an emotional setback when my daughter went out and purchased a housecoat identical to the one that was cut off me on the way to the ER. It was multiple shades of blue plaid with a cute little bow and snaps down the front. I know she meant well, but I could not bear to look at it. I tried to wear it but nearly had a full-on anxiety attack. Denise hid it. Maybe one day I will be able to wear it again.

Chapter 6

Heartbroken

May 2017. I got out of bed, came into the living room, and as usual turned on the news. It started off a day like any other day. Brandy and Denise were at work, and Billy was gone for the day. Denise got me my favorite breakfast, a sticky bun with walnuts. It was covered on a plate, patiently waiting for me on the stand by my chair. I got a cup of coffee and sat down to enjoy. I drank a bit of coffee, and after I ate about half of the bun, it felt like it was stuck in my throat. I could not swallow it. Then I started burping. Then came the throwing up. It got worse by the minute. Then my left arm suddenly felt like it was asleep, tingling with pins and needles. I called Brandy, and she came home. She said we should tell Denise and call an ambulance. Denise took one look at me and agreed it was time to go to St. Luke's, Allentown Campus. I decided that I would go, but I wanted her to drive me rather than call the ambulance.

When we arrived at St. Luke's, they took me right in and admitted me. Then came the blood work, EKG, physical exam, IV fluids, and nitro patch. Diagnosis: heart attack. Stable for now, I was moved to a regular room after several hours. After a flood of doctors, nurses, and aides, it was decided that a catherization would be needed the next day. Some sort of blockage might have been the culprit.

While we are very accustomed to lung issues and terminology, a heart attack was a shock, and there is quite a learning curve. I was very nervous and scared about the procedure; I was going to be put to sleep and experience the same issue as before, temporarily paralyzed on Propofol.

I headed down for the catherization, but the team put me at ease by telling me they would not use Propofol. It was a relief. They said they would go in through my wrist and fix any blockage they found. For some reason unknown to me, they had to go through my groin to complete the procedure. It was over quickly, and I went back to my room to endure the five hours of lying nearly flat on my back. This is not the most comfortable position for someone with breathing issues.

They did not in fact find a blockage, but to everyone's surprise, they found a tear where the left secondary artery branches off from the main coronary artery. A stent was impossible in that area because it ran the risk of tearing the artery further.

The area was hard to get at, and with my breathing being so bad and me being so weak from the issues in

February, my chances of surviving an open-heart surgery were not good. Two days later, they decided another catherization was needed to take more pictures and assess the situation more thoroughly. Even though I knew what was going on, having had the same procedure a few days before, I was still scared to be sedated again.

With me experiencing quite a bit of anxiety, the catherization team must have sensed my apprehension. When I was wheeled into the holding area prior to the procedure, the first member to the team remarked, "Didn't I see you here a couple times before? Don't believe what you hear. The tenth one is not free!" As the team members gathered around to move me from the bed to the operating table, the funny one continued. "Don't worry, we have not dropped a woman yet, but we did only have male patients today!" I was happy for the jokes because they really did cut down on my anxiety.

It did not take long before I was back in my room again. It had taken only an hour because they had gone in through the same groin location. When the doctor came in, he told us that the tear in my artery was starting to heal. So for right now we would see if medications would aid in my recovery. In three weeks, they would plan to do another catherization and see if it had healed further. Then we would decide what to do next. Most importantly, I had been put to sleep twice since February and had not heard a thing! So, yes, it was true. The fact that I could hear but not move before did not mean it would happen every time.

I also have not had any nightmares since I was released from the hospital this last time. I can be watching TV and think about all the things that happened to me. Of all the great things that I have experienced in my life—my wedding, the birth of my children and grandchildren, and even all the special moments spent with family and friends—for some reason this horrible memory is like poison ivy. When you have poison ivy, you cannot avoid the itching no matter what you do. It consumes your thoughts. The dark side still takes over my thoughts in those moments when I am relaxing with no task at hand to occupy me. I have been diagnosed with post-traumatic stress disorder (PTSD) from my horrifying experience that I cannot forget. This can happen to anyone of any age.

Today I sat down on my recliner to take a breathing treatment. I lay back and started the nebulizer. Thoughts came rushing back, and I remembered how terrifying the whole experience was. It made me think about the other people this might have happened to. I wonder if there were people who went through this and then passed away before realizing what happened.

I was informed by one of my doctors that hospitals are considering lowering the amount of anesthesia to cut the length of ICU recovery time. The more sedation medication they give you, the longer it takes for you to get back to feeling yourself. I am not sure if what happened to me was because of a fluke in my body, but I hope this would not result in other patients experiencing what I did.

Surely a few more days in ICU or recovering is better than having to relive this ordeal in the quiet moments. This is not something I would want anyone else to experience. My opinion is that dosing guidelines should not be inflexible; if you need more, why shouldn't the doctor give you what you need? On a side note, I wonder if a test of some sort exists to detect if you are "asleep" or just paralyzed?

I can stand now and even walk out onto my front porch on my own. I take deep breaths and smell the fresh air. I watch the birds and the neighborhood buzz with activity while enjoying a freshly brewed cup of coffee. After what I have been through, I learned not to take one moment of peace and happiness for granted. Now, I am off to spend every precious moment I have left with my

friends and loved ones.

.

Resources

For more information on Propofol:

www.pubmed.gov

www.drugs.com/propofol

www.fda.gov

Made in the USA
Lexington, KY
23 November 2019